Arik and Company

A Documentary Poem

Atar J. Hadari

Ben Yehuda Press
Teaneck, New Jersey

ARIK AND COMPANY ©2025 Atar J. Hadari All rights reserved. No part of this book may be used or reproduced in any manner whatsoever without written permission except in the case of brief quotations embodied in critical articles and reviews.

Published by Ben Yehuda Press
122 Ayers Court #1B
Teaneck, NJ 07666

http://www.BenYehudaPress.com

To subscribe to our monthly book club and support independent Jewish publishing, visit https://www.patreon.com/BenYehudaPress

Jewish Poetry Project #48   http://jpoetry.us

Ben Yehuda Press books may be purchased at a discount by synagogues, book clubs, and other institutions buying in bulk. For information, please email markets@BenYehudaPress.com

ISBN13 978-1-963475-56-2 pb 978-1-963475-57-9 epub

25 26 27 28 / 10 9 8 7 6 5 4 3 2 1a   250719

For Juliet

Who was born on the first day of Disengagement
On the floor of an Arab stone house
six feet inside the Green Line
in Jerusalem

And

For Gershom

Who said Sharon was the heart of darkness

Atar J. Hadari

Because massacres have known beginnings but not endings.
—Bayan Nuwayhed al Hut,
Sabra and Shatila, September 1982

Q: Whose life is better to tell the history of Israel, Arik Sharon or Shimon Peres?

A: It is much easier to write about bandits who shoot people with six-guns than about swindlers.

—Dialogue with historian Gershom Gorenberg concerning historical sources

Contents

Chronology / vii

Sticks / 4
A Knife in the Hand / 6
Latrun / 10
Before the First Battle / 12
David / 13
Examinations / 15
The Night In Question / 17
Margalit / 18
Step Into the Yard / 19
First Born / 20
Lily and the Suspect / 22
The Unexpected Caller / 23
Rabin / 26
Lawless in Gaza / 28
Inside Man / 29
Ants / 30
The Desert Rat / 31
Sand / 33
Sister / 34
Whenever / 36
Because / 37
Why / 39
Begin and Beauty / 40
The Word / 41
Eyewitness / 43
The Ship / 45
The Temple Mount / 47
The Explosion / 48
Barak / 50
Elyakim Rubinstein / 52
Bibi / 53

Why Then / 55
When / 56
Her Orange Hat / 57
A Family Picture / 58
The Feast / 59
Song of the Second Lebanon War / 60
Support / 61
Odysseus Rests / 62
Homage to Gilad Shalit / 63
Nobody Feeds the General / 65

Afterword: Telling Lies About the Dead / 67

Acknowledgments / 72
About the Author / 73

Chronology

1922   Shmuel Scheinerman elopes with medical student Vera Shneorov fleeing Communist revolutionaries hostile to his Zionist activity. Shmuel and Vera ship to Palestine with few possessions, settle in Kfar Mahlal, a socialist agricultural community, whose political outlook and joint agricultural policy they despise.

1926   Judith (Dita) Scheinerman born.

1928   Ariel Scheinerman born.

1934   At 6 Ariel's father gives him a stick and tells him to watch their fields so none of the neighbours steal their fruit.

1942   At 14 Ariel becomes an instructor in Gadna, a paramilitary youth movement, then joins the underground paramilitary Haganah, precursor to the IDF.

1948   Appointed platoon commander in the Alexandroni Brigade of the newly formed IDF. Severely injured in ambush at Battle of Latrun, attempting to free besieged Jews of Jerusalem. Broods in hospital over shortcomings of IDF command.

1950   Appointed intelligence officer for central command. Takes leave to study Middle Eastern culture at Hebrew University.

1951   Asked to form Unit 101, to retaliate against cross-border infiltration.

1953   Leads raid on Qubiyah after a Jewish mother and two children killed by a grenade thrown in their house. 69 Arab civilians are killed in the ensuing raid. International outcry. Meets Prime Minister Ben Gurion. Unit 101 merged with Paratrooper battalion, under the command of Ariel Sharon. (Ben Gurion advised him to Hebraize his name.)

1962   Margalit, first wife, killed in driving accident; he marries her sister, Lily.

1964   Promoted by Yitzhak Rabin to Chief Staff Officer at Northern Command.

1965   Promoted to General Headquarters and appointed Head of Training.

1967   Sharon's war plan rejected by PM Eshkol, then accepted by newly appointed Defence Minister Moshe Dayan. Conquest of Sinai makes Sharon a national hero.

1967	First son, Gur, killed playing with his father's gun with a friend.
1967	As Head of Training, begins Jewish settlement of West Bank by moving IDF training camps there.
1970	Appointed Head of Southern Command; launches war on terrorism in Gaza.
1972	Resigns from IDF and launches negotiations to form the Likud.
1973	Yom Kippur War. Sharon recalled to service; leads a division across the Suez Canal, narrowly averting a debacle. Meets Leonard Cohen, who is entertaining troops. Sharon's criticism of high command to US press leads to his removal from rank of division commander (reserve).
1975	Sharon leaves Likud to return to IDF as reserve commander.
1976	Crosses party lines to act as Special Advisor to PM Yitzhak Rabin. Presents plan to implement direct voting and give more power to PM.
1976	Announces formation of new party called Shlomzion.
1977	Begin invites Sharon to join the first Likud government as Agriculture Minister, Head of Ministers Committee for Settlement.
1978	Calls Begin at Camp David to urge uprooting Sinai settlement to gain peace.
1981	Appointed Defense Minister; instructs IDF to prepare Operation Peace in Galilee.
1982	Cabinet approves 40 km operation. IDF invades Lebanon.
1982	The newly elected Lebanese president Bashir Gemayel is assassinated on September 14th. IDF occupy Beirut. Phalange militia enter IDF-controlled Sabra and Shatila refugee camps and massacre Palestinian civilians.
1983	Kahan Commission find Sharon personally responsible; recommends he never serve as Defense Minister again.
1983	While cabinet debates the report, two demonstrations, one supporting and one opposing Sharon, converge on the building and a grenade is thrown into the Peace Now demonstration. Emil Grunzweig killed. Sharon asked to resign.
1983	Begin announces he cannot carry on and retires to his home.
1999	Ehud Barak, a sometime Sharon protégé, elected Prime Minister as heir of Rabin. Launches peace talks, which fail.
2000	Opposition leader Ariel Sharon visits Temple Mount sparking Intifada uprising.

2001	Elected Prime Minister.
2002	IDF attacks and bulldozes Jenin refugee camp.
2003	Re-elected Prime Minister with huge majority.
2003	Police investigations of Greek Isle affair corruption scandal begin.
2004	Sharon announces Disengagement Plan to unilaterally withdraw from Gaza.
2005	All Israeli settlements in Gaza and four in West Bank demolished. Only violent resistance is in Kfar Darom, where yeshiva students throw acid at IDF soldiers climbing to rooftop.
2005	Launches new party, Kadima, leading many Likud MKs to join.
2005	Suffers a stroke and is hospitalized in Shlomo Argov room, named after the ambassador to Britain whose attempted assassination sparked the Lebanon War.
2006	IDF soldier Gilad Shalit kidnapped by Lebanese militia. Sharon's replacement as PM, Ehud Olmert, launches Second Lebanon War. Commission of inquiry forces Defense Minister Amir Peretz to resign.

Arik and Company

Vera

She took out her loneliness
spread it like a deck of cards –
one was the Ace of Spades,
one the Jack of Hearts,
one was the picture of
where you meant to live
one the casually passed
word in the street
with a friend, a single friend –

She took out the pictures
and dealt them like hands –
lives she would have never had
wherever she walked, with whatever man

But under the pictures
always lurked the same baize
beneath the baize
the word that burned
from the lack of hands
to touch it, between games.

Sticks

His father taught him guarding fruit
was worth any number of lost friends
and fists clenched and unclenched –
sometimes never unclenched.

But he could take a punch just like a dog.
Kept the fat, to take whatever felt too intimate
too much like a kiss from the heart –
Just there and not too near.

When he was a kid
the punch used to roll through him like a wind
and fall away the other side.
He shook inside, like a dog's muscles glide

There was an echo like a sound
In the earth. That's when they told him to walk around
with a stick in his hand.
Speak softly wasn't mentioned.

He said to say it was for the wild dogs.
So many dogs snuffling the grapes.
He would hit anyone who wouldn't sit
And listen to what the class instructor said.

Today his dogs run around the farm.
Their flanks are soft as feathers
And roll like men under the sand
When you pull back the fetters.

They couldn't feel a punch
Even if you walked right up then delivered
Something you been saving for weeks.
They've got it down. Can't feel a thing.

All those days, walking without a stick
And then under the cover of nightfall
Then in broad daylight with a stick of dynamite
And no friends, watching for a snout

To come out of the brick, to pay back for it all.

A Knife in the Hand

They didn't say it wouldn't be mine.
Looking out the window of the cabin,
overboard at that unfolding shore,

I knew whatever I brought with me
when Shmuel whisked me away, and shouted "Marry me"
– whatever I managed to keep of medicine and bandages

was all I was going to get
there was no more of it here to be had,
this was the end of promises.

So we bought bad land. I acknowledge it.
We didn't have money. But we bought.
Whatever these swindlers thought

when we came and bought those shameful acres
that is what we bought.
And then to say – "But it's democracy.

Your husband wants to grow what? He's just crazy!"
If anybody may be foolish
it's me for being here to plant these oranges

Instead of in a white coat and stethoscope in Budapest
but let *me* say if my husband is nuts,
I may be mad but he knows about plants.

What is democracy? A bunch of strangers
forcing you to think what's not in your own hand.
I walked the wards, in Budapest, I smelt the gas,

they burned to boil the instruments,
they just about wore masks when I was trained
– I could have been a surgeon, I, the only girl

to wear a star of David in our whole part of the Pale
with not one Jew but our house in that bit of Mongol veil –
I was going to treat the lame and ill,

wear an icy gown
walk the ward and nod and frown –
I wanted it so much I still taste sweet

in the back of my throat, sometimes
when I wake up at midnight and the hiss
of laudanum, the fire under instruments boiled red

makes me dig nails into my palm –
I wanted it so bad I could have bled
from looking at those Jaffa shacks on the shore

and I did not come here and give all that up
to be told by some socialist whose land
will be given away as a free gift to new inhabitants.

So they had a vote? So what?
So they said the village votes to donate land.
Did *I* say I'd give up some dirt? Who bothers to raise a hand

when the party owns all the hands that count?
So I went out, at midnight, I admit it,
I ran barefoot to the fence post

where the line-man stretched his spool of tin –
and I cut it – I made an incision, I'm not ashamed –
– in two places – wire shone in the moon like a jagged vein

down an old lady's collar bone
where the knife can slip under the wrinkled skin –
I used to be the one holding the blade,

if Shmuel had waited till I wore my graduation gown
to get scared and run out of Poland
I'd have been a qualified surgeon

a potentate
not some thief who has to steal the air to breathe.
Next day the line-man came and knocked

he says, "Your husband in?"
"Away," I say, "paying the loan
for this land, working other people's farms."

Those bastard socialists wanted to give our land
Away but would not waive one *grush* of loan.
We bought the land all right, just not a say in how things run.

"Funny thing," he says, "I stretched the line
across your land last night. Right through to where you planted ..."
"Rhubarb." "Rhubarb? ...Interesting. In any event,

the wire fell-down, in two places,
Right where it meets the fence in fact.
Exactly as if cut, a perfect slit."

"Do you think it was a good clean cut?" I said.
He looked at me. "Who made that cut can shave me any day."
So we're talking. I tell him about Shmuel's new ideas in fruit,

About the leper wards, the syphilis,
the world that's gone and never will repeat
and he says, shyly, "I did come
from the old country with a small problem."

He was a shtetl boy, turns out,
run off from the yeshiva bench to find
exactly what it is boys usually do find

when they run off with one thing on their mind.
So I told him *peni-ci-llin*.
They were prescribing that when I was first trained, just.

Atar J. Hadari

I know a syphilitic can touch a girl again.
He can go back if he wants, to that yeshiva bench.
Not like a woman with a son

who threw off her white coat and bought the land.
He didn't mention that cut wire again.
We parted like the best of friends.

And while the village had a lot of plots
that much smaller, ours, has stayed just the same.
A little bigger now than those Socialist plots with their heroic names.

I treasure it, that time, I got to feel what I could still have been –
getting a patient to open up
takes more than a white gown –

and I walk in the orange buds
and smell the instruments that cut and hear the roar
of all those tiny flaming heads and spread my hands into the clouds

and feel the hot breath of the fruit
and know I will not give an inch of this
before the surgeon comes to take my youth.

Latrun

(Yaakov Bogin)

Why I saved him I don't know.
A funny looking fat kid with no friends.
Used to come to scout meetings with a stick
for the coyotes. We'd see coyotes
maybe once in five years.
But he always knew his way in the dark.
And he never showed fear.
Once we started running around like tin soldiers
they all liked the fat kid.
And I never minded what his parents
grew on their cabbage patch.
So in Latrun I dragged him back.
Yeah, I took him on my back.

Another guy, from our same hole
in the ground, came and looked him in the eye,
looked at how much blood he lost,
the hole between his heart and belt
and said, well, he never said,
he just turned and left. Arik said he understood.
I've never noticed how he understood troops being late
on the parade ground, I don't know
how much he really *understands*.
But I just thought, "This man doesn't die.
I do not let this man lose what he has."
I saw something in him? After the fact, you know,
you can say you never minded
if he didn't pay you back
the two lira or the half falafel
but it wasn't like that.
I thought he had a gift.
And gifts you don't leave for Arabs to cut in half.
What wasn't cut in half by the rain
of bullets. So I said I would be a man.
They ran past us, the others, stopped sometimes then ran
and we hobbled, crawled, dragged

but I got him back to what we call Israel.
I wonder sometimes what would've happened to us all
if I had fallen down and left him out there?
Just a piece of metal on some meat
no Sinai campaign, no Lebanon, no Disengagement –
but then I think, Thank God for him –
if he hadn't been lying there half dead
I would've had to drag myself
and myself, maybe, I wouldn't drag.

Before the First Battle

Sticks got off lorries
sticks in old boat clothes,
European belts and jackets,
concentration camp blousons;

they were white and skeletal
as men still moving can be
and shucked off their European rags
to put on Israeli green to die;

loose belts, ballooning pants,
shirts like tents over their hearts,
they picked their guns – those that had guns –
and carried them like sticks of pine –

the men he watched, lying
on his stomach on the hot ground
soaking noonday heat,
letting it fill his skin and blood –

men he saw, nearly dead but full of strange
survival craft, the sort of hounds
that had survived a sinking raft,
the sort of men who should not have been found

strapping themselves into ill-fitting boots,
harnessing up World War One Turk issue guns
saying, "Wherever we have come from
we'll die as Jews, not without bearing arms."

He dropped back to sleep
the crickets shimmered in the hours,
night came slowly on its paws
and sank its teeth into all those wilted flowers,
red rags in its jaws.

Atar J. Hadari

David

1953 (Ben Gurion, PM 1948-1953)

He came to me, said his name was Scheinerman: "Nice man."
I said I needed someone to end these raids by Bedouin.
Arabs were using Jordan like a train station
And we were losing dozens, houses going up in flames.

He'd done things, had recommendations from people I heard of.
I asked him who they voted for where he came from.
"My father's neighbours all vote Labour."
And his friends? "Good boys. I was in the Palmach, like everyone."

At least he wasn't Begin's apprentice, killing civilians.
"And what will you do when you get across?" "Sir," he replied,
"General Dayan gives orders without using details.
He says it should be done. I let him know it's been handled…"

"You need a Hebrew name," I said,
"Scheinerman, – it should become handsome,
Why don't you call yourself Sharon?
Call yourself that and go out with a Unit called 101."

He touched his hat as he went out.
I was away on vacation
when he went on that famous mission.
Nobody asked me, though I dare say I would not have vetoed.

I went on air to say the government knew
nothing about it. The IDF were nowhere near
That village or any Arab's hairline
That may have been singed. Immigrants,

Middle-Eastern, emotional types – got
A bit out of hand seeking vengeance.
Natural, in the tragic circumstance.
A lie can sometimes be a thing sent from heaven.

The UN condemned and so did Switzerland.
But we had quiet for a while and blood of mothers
Stopped rattling around the Knesset cafeteria.
You could hear your tea in your tea-cup.

He touched his hat with a smile,
I wrote his name down: "Could go far,
If he learns not to lie."
You can't blame me for being half wrong.

What you get from such a man,
Is an entirely different matter.

Examinations

(Wars of Attrition 1956)

There've always been questions about Arik.
As far back as '52 when a night patrol
Spotted figures crossing the sand dunes.
Arik told his men to open fire, ask questions later.

The bodies turned out to be two Bedouin women with baskets.
He was fine. He smiled. He was Arik.
He's a man who cultivates friends.
I mean, what is a leader?

The week before Kibiyeh
We went out on another mission.
Three platoons, three different targets.
One was to go in an Arab village all guns blazing,

Scare the population. I got up and said, "You can't do that.
Those are innocent civilians."
He said, "You don't like it, don't go on that one.
Go on any one you like." By a miracle
There were no casualties.

Next week I saw my friend Falach, putting on dynamite.
Pound after pound of the stuff round his waistline,
In the end he looked like Arik:
A little man in the middle of a ball of sugar and sulphide.

Arik said to me, "You weren't here in the beginning.
The first mission I almost didn't go on.
I had a Middle East history exam.
The brigade commander said to me,

"Arik, some people study history,
some have the chance to do what will be studied."
We didn't blow up a fucking thing.
Got spotted on our way out of the village.

Arik and Company

Not enough dynamite to blow the shit arsonist's door.
Woke up the village, made so much noise
but all got back in one piece.
That's not the kind of mission we run these days."

"What's your exam in?" he said.
"Proper Legal Procedure."
"Go sit your exam," he said,
"Let me worry about the future."

The Night In Question

We reached the village by moonlight,
The loud speaker was crackling,
We said they should clear each house,
A lot left, I wasn't counting.

We found a boy in the street.
Didn't touch him, gave him a Bazooka
Bubble gum and showed him where to run
So he wouldn't get caught in the fiesta.

I went in one house myself.
There was a little girl in there crying.
Told her not to be upset,
She would find her Mummy and Daddy in the morning.

Took her by the hand myself.
Followed the boy with the Bazooka down the alley.
Then we started doing what we did.
In every house we stepped in, called "Out!" and put the charges in.

Next morning I was told some people hid in cellars.
68 bodies is a lie. I don't believe there ever
Could have ever been that many there.
A perfectly professional mission.

I tell you there's a little boy and girl
Who have good reason to remember my name.
In the morning they told me: Prime Minister on the phone.
At least we went out with a bang on our last mission.

Arik and Company

Margalit

(1st wife, married 1953)

Her husband came back from the attack
wading through stretchers like seed beds –
the dead and the wounded laid out like rags
and him straddling the concrete in giant steps –
staggering, sauntering, tired
but singing, not even out of breath
and she knew there would never be
a farmer's wife in the mirror
when she put on the bathroom light.
The roses when he came home
sometimes would age and wither,
would crumble on the wax table cloth
and blow away finally like a dry river –

then he'd be home again,
five hours, telling tales like an old sea dog
and then the nights and the endless flights
of stairs at the hospital
with no-one at home to tell about the detail.

One time she brought him round
to the patients, to look in on her ward –
she said, "Just talk to them"
and he stared and stared
as if they were an alien
unconquerable bit of sand.

Long nights and no fights
and long heroic rambles
when he came home and fell asleep
in the middle of re-capturing someone.

Step Into the Yard

1962

On the road to Jerusalem from Tel Aviv
where tanks would be displayed,
burnt out guns rust slowly away,
Margalit drove slowly, carefully

she veered to the right
for a few seconds and that day
brought her into a lorry
that sent her up to Shaarei Tzedek.

They comforted him,
"Judging by the remains
She could not have seen
Even a moment's anguish."

He read words over her from a folded piece
of paper and did not crack,
but towers did not rise from embers.
He took Lilly to music, steaks and galleries Margalit had wanted

and in the night rose like a ghost
to change the babies, wait for another conflict.
Margalit's boy Gur grew tall as a willow
and delicate as she had been, but full of power.

First Born

When Margalit died, Lilly moved in.
She never had much time for the man
("You married him? He knows a word that isn't gun?")

Now there was a noble cause,
a boy who didn't know about his mother,
("Where is she? When is she coming home?")

Opinionated, nervous, jumps like a scorched cat,
Lilly was all her sister was with added crackle.
They moved to a house, Arik came from base to shuck his khakis,

Ride the truck with Gur who grew up gangly as an ear of corn,
the girls and boys, they'd ring him round
– Arik looked on and glowed like a sea lion.

Arik was given a gift, a Turkish gun
that he hung on the mantle.
Gur's friend came by the house to play,

the friend took down the Turkish gun
and said they ought to find something to stuff the barrel.
Lilly came after half an hour

Arik was on the phone. The boys stepped out into the yard.
Arik was winding up and heard a pop,
ran out into the brambles, Lilly pulled into the forecourt,

Arik running with Gur in his arms,
to the doctor's clinic,
where they said "The hospital! The hospital!"

He got there in time for Gur to die
Spread out across his arms.
The nation came. There was word on the radio

thousands spared an hour to share the general's ruin.
Looking out the car window
He saw a man he'd never met before:

Menachem Begin: lantern jaw,
glasses of coal round eyes of cooling metal
and in them plain for anyone to see

the pain of seeing anybody lose a son
let alone a son
born after many sacrifices.

Standing over Margalit's grave
he remembered what he said
when he put up her stone: "I'll watch for Gur."

He lied. Now in the fresh grave
were two pieces of a life barely begun
to visit with a watering can.

Now there would always be images
of Gur riding or standing in the sun
in Arik's mind and he would sit and let them pass

like shadows on the plain
until he could again see glass
empty above the rim of the reflecting depths.

Lily and the Suspect

1963

She gave up on those life drawing classes.
You have to have a feel for it,
How a body hangs, how it feels force.
How a person holds their pockets

She couldn't ever get that.
Went to the police examination.
Gave up the class and took the cash
For sketching suspects from descriptions.

When they came to report a crime
She was there with a pencil.
No bodies, just faces from their words
When she got a nose right they'd shout, "That's it! That's it!"

It was much quicker to satisfy
Than bodies on a canvas.
If they get hold of him, maybe
He wouldn't kill somebody.

You can't tell what stopping
Someone doing something will do after all.
Like listening to Arik,
She prefers to hear, to sit right there.

Not wait until he leaves, calls.
So she goes along, does her drawings,
Makes things change. She got the music.

Quail wings, murmurs in the ear
When Margalit got the long night
Waiting up late. Life isn't fair.

When Arik comes she tells him
What they each did, who they murdered.
He knows just what to do with every one of them.
He wouldn't have a moment's hesitation.

Atar J. Hadari

The Unexpected Caller

1967

Rabin, general Chief of Staff
presented his plan – to take just half of Sinai,
up to El Arish and Gaza.
Arik called it piss poor fighting.

"We can crush the entire Egyptian tank force,
rush across the dunes and watch sunrise
over all of Sinai in our sweaty little hands."

Rabin was silent like a pot boiling.
Eshkol said "Not a whisper
To anyone outside this room."

Rabin took to bed with nerves,
Eshkol went on the radio, stuttered something,
Made everyone across the country shudder
like a lightning rod.

Arik whispered into Rabin's ear:
"Declare martial law."
Rabin got out of bed pronto;

Sharon went to his own base
locked himself up in a camper van
Pored over maps of Sinai,

Played out scenarios, cut and thrust –
Come morning he'd a plan for his division
To do all the miles under the sun.

An unexpected caller, former Chief of Staff, Moshe Dayan
Stopped by to ask what was on his tiny mind,
Listened and nodded, said, "I'll ride with you In the first column."

Two days later it was headlines
Dayan was Defence Minister
In coalition with Levi Eshkol.

Another meeting with the brass
this time Dayan in Levi Eshkol's chair.
He said "Fine", gave the go ahead to Arik's Sinai plays,

Arik briefed his ranks till half past ten
Then lay down between two half-tracks;
Got up fresh as a rose before the dawn:

His tank crossed the border before nine.
The tracks got buried in the sand.
His men crossed last miles in their boots

To lie buried in wait behind Egyptian lines.
At ten to twelve Arik ordered open fire.
The sky turned white as chalk
Arik pulled up next to his chief gunner:
"I've never seen a hell like this before."

Arik ordered buried troops to break cover –
They rose out of the dunes
And fell on the Egyptians like locusts:
A thousand lights ran through the sand
Rumbling like angry herons:

Egypt lost a thousand men,
History does not record how many lost limbs.

Arik declared the battle won at 3 am;
It was over just after ten
Arik's soldiers sleep inside their tanks
Under the noonday sun.

Over the radio Arik listened
As his old division, paratroopers,
Streamed into Jerusalem.
"That should have been me," he muttered

Then fell asleep over a feast
Of canned beef, chocolate and bourbon
Looted from an Egyptian army base
Full of dead men.

He went home and the papers
Called him the hero of El Arish;
He told her about the white sands of Rafah,
"It's all, all of it ours"

And fell asleep again
In a new land as fat as his middle;
As if the whole world were in his hand,
And would not ever want to fight again

Let alone with the new IDF head of training
Who loved every grain of sand
And knew just where to put each training camp
To grow the chance for peace.

Rabin

1967
(Yitzhak Rabin, Chief of Staff, later PM)

You've got no tact
To play a part
In any joint decision;

You've got no heart
For staying out
Of any bit of action.

You do not listen.
When a military policeman
Tells you "no can do."

You do not show any discipline,
Chew him out
In front of your battalion,

Make sport of his private life,
Walk, limp, receding hairline.
These things don't go unmentioned
When it comes to discussing promotion.

How you talk does not improve the situation.
When you go behind his back
Or over his head to the kitchen cabinet

Because you have Ben-Gurion's private line
Or some other way to get your own back
It isn't in your own interest.

Every time you get your way
Another enemy is waiting
For the right moment.

The army is like playing chess
You need to see
Where pawns are waiting

To take your Queen.
Now Ben Gurion is gone
Who will you go to, to let you win?

Who can you call, when your latest plan
Is foiled because the next man up the totem pole
Remembers what you mean by discipline?

You'll never make a good officer
You do not have the patience.
I'm giving you Southern Command.
Get out of here. Prove me mistaken.

One day you might have the chance
To be a man
Instead of talking to the mountains.

On that day remember me.
You do not always have to win
To be a good statesman.

Lawless in Gaza

We used to have a lot of trouble in lawless Gaza.
Then Arik took over the Southern Command.
He was a hot shot, y'know, Unit 101, the Paratroops,

But we still thought, "He's just one man. Harmless.
What's he going to do in Sodom and Gomorrah."
Well, he came and he took command, nothing

He thought about it and he made a new ruling.
Any Arab found with a gun
Would be shot on the spot without warning.

It got quiet after a while.
I think of that when they say
He made enemies.

Hasn't ever been the same
Since he went down to Jerusalem.
It still gets quiet here after a big car bomb.

Don't get me wrong, he made mistakes
But you could hear yourself think
With a gun in your hand.

Now you run for your life.
Now I don't know, he was right, he was wrong.
I do what I'm ordered.

But when I look out in the night
I wish he was still on the road.
I'd take the consequences.

I live with myself.
But as it is now, there is no law
And we are the wolves.

Inside Man

1973

I like quiet, music, landscapes, friends.
I'm not made to manipulate crowds.
It's true with a bloody bandage on my head
I make a good photograph.

But I don't speak like a political animal,
I talk like somebody who acts.
You want to influence from outside
You have to speak, like Menachem Begin does.

I went and sailed the world,
Everywhere I went I said nice things.
Only in Israel I wasn't meant to land.
But I remained inside. Up in the air

When the Egyptians came in '73
They washed the sand away with water hoses.
By then I was campaigning for myself,
for the Likud, but I still could be persuasive

With a gun in my hand, or at least a siren
making everybody listen,
like a radio announcing casualties.
when our trucks came and went listlessly

Across the silver glints of the canal
They didn't fire at us, Egyptians
They must have known, deep in their britches,
We came right back where we had been missing.

Ants

1973
(Menachem Begin, PM 1977-1982)

He came to me, said he wanted to form this new
right-wing party of parties. Likud he called it.
I knew him – who didn't know him?
We did talk once upon a time –
When he was going to walk out on the army.
But I didn't swoon then, and he didn't walk away from the army.
This time was different. He had arithmetic.
Said if the little right-wing parties made a big block
Ben Gurion and his lot would be out on their ears,
That got me to sit up and listen. He had a farm by then
Going back and forth planting his acres
Then coming back, hammering out a platform
For these ants to come together one by one to make a wedding cake,
Each with their own sweet crumb. I was the cherry.
If he got me to be the fruit on top, he had a party.
I did not break his hand in the rush to shake it.
I took my time, considered facts, kept looking at his feet under the table.
He had big feet in fat sandals, dripping with arable.
Underneath every toenail at least an inch of holy soil
Off the land of Israel. He'd ploughed or stomped or fed the animals
Before he came to the table. I signed. Did I know what would happen?
He was not the demobbed general, I was not the rookie party animal –
He was saying something new, changing the lay of the periodic table.
I loved the notion of a born Hebrew soldier
Who would let you know where you were.
Then we won. And there my troubles began.
Who knew it was so hard to keep every single marble?

The Desert Rat

(Leonard Cohen, 1973 Yom Kippur War)

I took my Bhagavad Gita
my acoustic and my shout
and went aboard the plane
saying, in Jerusalem I will not touch
a single girl except in love,
And I descended into Tel Aviv
To test my new resolve.

There is nothing more appealing to your senses
Than those sure economic movements,
Of a country in a state of war –
I boarded a lorry straight to the Sinai desert
and me and this curly youth with a steel guitar
drove the burning asphalt
and wherever we saw soldiers we just stopped
and sang – it was the purest form of show business.
I could not help but see soldiers undressed.
Those girls in green and grey and navy
Waving like hula skirts in the breeze,
then the lorries took us across Suez
To the Desert Rat, general Sharon's headquarters.

He was sitting in the outskirts of a base he cleared
with a can of beans that said, "Gift of the Canadian Mounties."
He offered me a sip of something hard,
A corner of his shade next to a half track.
I said, "How dare you?" but he showed no sign of remorse
Just grinned and asked me how I liked my steak burned.
He had hair white as a lamb even then.
and a bandage across his brow where a beam caught it.

Golda Meir was not taking his calls. A new thing for him,
Since youth he'd always been able to reach
Israel's Prime Minister without intermediaries. It hurt his feelings.
I told him about the Bhagavad Gita, where the general stands
and sees the front line on the other side,
former teachers, friends and he's all ice until the manifest hand

of the deity, in Krishna, speaks to him:
"You were brought here by me,
They died before the sun started burning, you too have died already.
Millions of men have already been born, died and do not yet know it,
It is not you who brought your steps here, but me
Now rise, and be a man –"

He laughed and the desert wind ruffled stray strings on his bandage.
I said I couldn't sing except on twelve-year-old Scotch
And for fifteen-year-old girls.
I left my wife when I got back from the war.
He left the army, I'm not sure who lost their way.
They took him back. I just took the Rock and Roll Hall of Fame
and made them listen to me read Verlaine.
I took the desert with me back to the rain.
The sun never came out of that acoustic.
It's still a little grainy when I tune it.
You can hear that can of beans and wine and someone singing in the ruins,
But nobody can ever tell me again a tank can't be a shelter for a poet.

Sand

1977

In 1977 Arik with two seats
to his one-issue party
re-joined Likud's Begin
as Minister of Settlement and Housing.

A tiny flaw arose
since Arik owned one of the largest
privately held plots in Israel
there could be a perceived conflict of interest.

Arik gave half the farm to Lilly.
Lilly opined: "You can't make someone give up his way of living."
Four farmers leased the farm from Arik
for the duration of his office term.

Finally in 1980 Motti
Arik's driver in the Yom Kippur debacle
created a company that leased the farm
and grew the same array of wool and cattle.

A few months later the press discovered
the state sold a hundred and twenty-three acres
to Arik's driver. Minister Sharon
was the richest man in Israel
in privately owned grains of sand.

Sister

I saw him coming around this glass,
Saw him through that courtyard in the snow
Fifteen security men with walkie talkies stomped
On the azaleas, my mother would've had him stoned.

I let him in, didn't let security inside the door.
Let them freeze their asses on the flowers.
He walked the two flights. There was no lift.

Then he came, stood there where you were.
We looked at each other. Kiss?
We didn't come from that kind of house.
He sat right there where you are sat.

Did I give him cake? He was big as a moose,
Why should I feed the son of a bitch?
We drank cold soda, just like the old days.
Out of a bottle. I fill them with gas.

But he looked good. Fat, but good.
A little puffy round the eyes, a bit fish pale.
Not too much riding around on tractors
No matter what the cameras tell.

Who would have imagined,
He actually left the old man
Behind, for all that he got the farm.
Actually went to work in town.

Do I resent it? Not being left a dunam,
Not an inch, an acre of my father's land?
Twenty-five thousand dollars my mother left
From an estate worth I forget how many million.

Fourteen point one. No, I don't bear a grudge.
He put up with her. He drove her here and there.
He did not marry someone they didn't care for.
Anyway, she died. Then he took her sister.

That was Biblical. They couldn't say boo to that.
So, he got all the dirt. The flowers, rhodedendrons.
Fruit trees, farm, and the chest full of vegetables.
How he got away from the old man I'll never know.

We discussed it, amicably.
I asked if he'd give a little,
An acre of dirt for my little girl
To have something my parents loved –

He wouldn't hear of it.
"They gave what they could give," he said.
He went out and left a ring on that table
Where the glass of water stood.

A little halo of cold water.
He was gone and all the azaleas mud.
But he looked well. I couldn't begrudge him
Every atom of dirt they ever farmed.

I left that country and every cloud they leeched from
Now what I see is snow that I can grind
Until it's only gas – and I can give my child
Something that will not blind them.

There is no land around here not worth
More to somebody without the urge to die.

Whenever

Whenever some turbulent side
of this emaciated state goes up in fires,
we all say "Why do we lead this life?"
then send Arik with a knife.

Whenever somebody mentions wrong
or flashes pictures of the Viet Cong
in massacres and says "How long?"
we all remember Arik's damned.

Whenever some parade goes by
and Hawks like pigeons dot the sky
and no-one wonders what's the time
we all cheer every Arik line.

Whenever some battle got lost
or a big river got won at cost
or someone said they never built it
we all remember – Arik did it.

Because

September 1982, Sabra and Shatila

I have attempted to record a massacre.
Because the telling of massacres is secret.
It goes on in the blood which dries
As well as in the bones in ditches.
Because massacres need re-telling
and go on and on being told especially in silence,
it is the particular provenance
of massacres to be told in the lack of utterance.
Because there is no way to end a story
Which does not stop for telling.
Because the dead do not return
Except each night when darkness is spreading.
Because of the dryness
Of the blood which is not flowing,
Blood on the handkerchiefs
And pillows and streets and the curls
Of a boy who will not grow to bear witness –

Because the told will not stay uttered
But rings and writhes in ear holes,
Blood will not stay anywhere but in gutters
It rattles and rings in the piers and against pillars,
Blood will upset apple carts and records,
Blood injects pupils in eyes with roses
To colour fear on every white pearl
Open bloody sheets on every citadel –

When the storm stops, and floods fill all the thimbles.
Because I believe that just
What is written can hold the silence,
Because there is no rest
From the voices in the cold at night
That say there is something that must be reckoned
Before they find their resting place
But what that is they do not know,
So I say what they did instead.

Why

1982
(Yehoshua Saguy, Assistant Head Military Intelligence –1979-83)

They asked me why I couldn't say
What I said to the soldiers, to the statesmen,
Why as Israel's Chief of Intelligence
I could not open my mouth and spill the beans,
That we were going to get slaughtered.

I was at the General Staff Meeting where Minister Sharon
Outlined Big Pines, I was at the Cabinet
When Sharon described his 40 kilometres strike.
I told them, "nothing will come of this but blood on your head."
Like water on a fireplace.
I knew every word out of his mouth
Was spinning like a plate on a bamboo cane.
Even if he had not yet dropped the match in his hand
It was already a live, moving thing,
More than I could swallow and still stand.

If I had said – who would have listened?
Soldiers who will bleed,
Generals who had their best friend's
Spleen across their shirt,
All would have said, "So?"
So Begin I should tell, or at least the rest?
Begin at least killed somebody,
One time, the rest had no idea.

Silence, like a wall of flame
Around him, I could see Beirut
Exploding as he spread his fingers
Across the map and said: "So far. No more—"

The crows flew round and round inside his head
And I could not stop their cawing
No matter what I said or never said.
There was no stopping the inferno.

Begin and Beauty

Menachem Begin lived like vermin
Until nineteen forty eight
Then after evading assassination
Survived an enemy of the state
Unmentioned in government motions,
Unnamed, unaddressed in debate,
Until a serpent in robes of emerald
Suggested a greater fate.
He took power in seventy seven
And ruled like a potentate:
Tried to exercise restraint,
A model of modest taste.
He had only this one weakness
And made it Minister of Defence.
He loved the sons of Judean dirt
Who never bowed a knee even when beat.
And this weakness said, "Forty kilometres.
Into Lebanon. What could be wrong with that?"
And that was the end of Menachem Begin.
Sometimes vermin last more than lions.
Except lions who know not to trust
A creature that kills not for food
But for the beauty of the hunt,
The relentless chase after the hart.

The Word

1983 (The Kahan Commission)

The Minister of Defence bears personal
Responsibility for the massacre,
While not being directly responsible
He is indirectly responsible.

By not anticipating acts
By others – which were not unforeseeable
He in his negligence endangered lives
Of many civilians.

Members of the commission
Expect him to draw his own conclusions.

It is not considered the Prime Minister
Or other members
Knew what they were doing.

With regard to the Minister of Defense
That cannot be the conclusion.

We expect him to draw his own conclusions
And do what is expected of him.

In the desert something moving
Gathers speed near Bethlehem.

A thousand feet and no face in the sun,
No arms and no pinions
Just footprints and blood and the shame
And not a soul to say anything.

Not a soul left with a tongue still in its jawbone.
After the screams have died down,
The paper notes have flown,
The men walking from the courtroom

Dry their hands,
And one man left inside
Holding the table like a strand
As the sea leaves him behind

Just one prophet, a photographer
Said, "Who did not let him serve as Chief of Staff
Got him as Minister of Defence.
Who doesn't want him Minister of Defence
Will see him Prime Minister."

But nobody listens to prophets.

Eyewitness

For G. G.

I was there with the marchers.
While the mob brayed "Arik Melech Yisrael"

I was running a fever,
And the rain came pummelling,

So I tendered my excuses to the revolution,
Went home – only time in my life.

It was only when I dragged myself
To bed, switched on the radio

I heard somebody threw
a grenade into the middle of the demo.

Emil Grunzweig lost his life.
That was when Begin made him resign.

He was his blue-eyed boy.
The native Hebrew warrior.

All that diaspora generation,
They built the country but they weren't born here.

Sharon was born here.
It killed Begin making him resign.

Sometimes I think Emil's still in that square
Asking for the price of a falafel.

I can't go by Zion Square without remembering Sharon
And how my life was saved by an infection.

Only that boy with his eyes blown out
Got that maniac thrown out of the cabinet.

Atar J. Hadari

The Ship

1983
(Menachem Begin, PM 1977-1983)

The ship came in beyond the break
It pushed away waves like snowflakes.
Then the firing started.
The Prime Minister didn't understand.
I said give me twenty percent
Of arms for my own regiment.
For *Jerusalem*, for heaven's sake,
Apparently, that got his goat.
"Army within an army" or some such rot.
To me he said not a word.
Nor a whisper, not a look.
Said my request would be *reviewed*.
Next thing we knew there was fire at us from the sand.

We'd signed an armistice ten days before.
The Irgun and Ben Gurion's lot, all Jews
Were all one army – mine, his, every gun
In the land except the ones at sea
That I'd paid for with my own funds.
That made my blood fair game, apparently
A small price to be paid
As it had been for years
Since I blew up the King David.

Arik, I'll tell you the truth,
If I could have had the Prime Minister's head
On a plate with an apple in his mouth
And a glaze like honey over his ears
I wouldn't have done it. I don't eat pig.
I ordered my men not to fire back,
Because Jews do not kill Jews, Arik,
I will not be the cause.
I spilled out words all night
Over the radio from an Irgun house,
Told the good people of Tel Aviv he was a louse

But did not say to touch a hair on his hand.
I sat in the Knesset ranks
While he made this land sand.
He would not even say my *name*.
For twenty-seven years I was
"The member sitting next to Asher K."

Now I am the one with the phone
Saying, "We will do this, do that"
And they listen. Only you do not.
I thought you did. I thought I heard

Every movement the army made.
Thought the eagle was trained to my hand.
Now I find it flies its own way.
What is it about this land?

Arik, it was a sight, that ship.
Nobody got onto land,
It was empty and burning by the end.
Bodies in the water, guns in the sand.
Women standing on the street outside now
Shout we're murderers. Child-killers. Signs
Say how many killed, and they chorus
"Killer, Killer, Killer" wherever I go out.

I took the fire on deaf ears.
Hunted by Arabs, British, Jews
I do not have another life to give.
When there are Jews saying you're the devil
You must change your way of life.

I knew my part was silence
When the ship burrned
Like an athlete's torch,
Now do you know yours?
I started this country with my silence.
Will you let it be torn to shreds?
Why should it wait until tomorrow for you to resign?
I was gone before the fire was ash.

The Temple Mount

2001

At a scheduled walkabout
On the Temple Mount
By the leader of the opposition

Palestinians threw cocktails
In a spontaneous outbreak of demonstration.

Riots spread all over the nation.
There were elections.

The Peace process was abandoned.
There was a change of direction.

The Explosion

In the early twilight or late tea-time
They left the clinic, he had his coat on.
He stopped on Jerusalem high road
And bought two strudels in a carton.
They went to the new cafe,
A father, his daughter, her best friend
Who was going to hold the bride's bouquet

And put her make-up on the next day.
They squeezed in past the guard
Who was Russian and didn't speak Hebrew,
Went up to a table with a hoard
Of sugar lumps and cups white as a swallow,
As he was ordering two lattes, one black tea
He heard the Russian utter something:
A man in a heavy woollen coat
Put his hands to the windowpane
And pushed through in a cascade of smithereens
To pull something inside his blouson
And the cafe went up, you could hear a mile off.
As if a paper lantern rose into the air to float on
And cross the sky over a wedding feast.

Merciful father who dwells on high
Furnish a rest fitting
Under the wings of the divine presence
For those who die innocent of trespass –

The nurse at the clinic called and called
And called his mobile.
Next day the guests were told
One by one, not to come for the nuptial.
But all reported at twilight
Seeing walking along the pavement
As if underneath their feet
The sun had beat a golden raiment
One old man, a girl, another girl, all in white satin
And in the old man's hand a box, immeasurably comforting

And tied with ribbons and not crushed,
Under their feet gold flashed without saying anything.
Just the carton full of pastry in his hand that would not be eaten by anyone.

Barak

(PM 1999-2001)

I first met Arik when I was a platoon commander punk.
He was head of Southern Command.
My unit was exercising reconnaissance,
We had to get in his base and get out.
I led the platoon under cover of dawn,
We were over the fence, down the hall.
I left him a note in his desk drawer
With regards from a girl he used to know.
He laughed himself sick hearing how we slipped his guard.
A couple years later my name came up
For promotion – a general's star.
I had every medal going but was not a company man.
There were objections from people below,
Above– I should not hold that rank.
Arik was then – minister of defense? I don't know.
Maybe they thought he knew all about
Someone who paid no attention to what they were told.
He recommended my appointment.
Remembered my note in his desk drawer.
For years the Labour Party chased
After a general with balls enough to make peace.
I tried, I failed. I shook hands
With Arafat but no-one believed
The deal we made would stick.
At least I wasn't shot like Rabin.
I called the country back,
Just to make
Sure we were all on the same tack.
Arik was leader of the opposition,
Nobody thought he'd ever make PM.
I called an election, Arik pounced.
A two hundred pound silver mountain lion
Laughing himself sick as he flies through the air.
He called a press conference to watch him walk
A grandfatherly stroll round the Al-Aksa mosque –
The grandfather who can make peace
But with security had to set foot

On the Temple Mount. The Palestinians
Took my offer of more square feet
Than any Israeli government ever dreamed to relinquish
And threw Molotov cocktails at his feet.
Exquisitely shod feet, may I add,
He was no longer the farmer boy Begin admired.
A beautiful suit, white hair, wry smile.
Molotovs flew like sunflower seed
Shells through the Temple yard.
Within six weeks I was out.
What Arik gave, Arik took away. I learned hard,
You had to listen more than shout.
Arik became what they always said he wouldn't,

That's why I tell you, young men,
Don't be smart. If they ask you to break in
To the devil's office, say no thank you,
Because the boring path will kill you
But you'll have your dreams –
If you let the devil kiss you
You'll have eternity to see
How little you are in his schemes.

I had to persuade my secretary
To stay and work for him.
"I can't work for a man like that."
"You can. You will. He's not like you think.

You can't leave all of us
Without a grown-up looking after him.
Don't let anyone get at his desk either.
We'll never hear the end of them."

Elyakim Rubinstein

I asked the retired Attorney General
To compare the present incumbent
To the Prime Minister he had served,
Yitzhak Rabin, who had refused his resignation.

He said, "Rabin was a different animal.
He used to blush when he said something inaccurate,
That redhead with a redhead's temperament
Used to turn the colour of beetroot."

Bibi

PM 1996-1999
Minister of Finance 2003-2005

Bibi, come in, take a load off,
You're looking good – lost a little weight?
You don't look like me, behind this desk.
You get to run around, on the ground, smell blood.
You know exactly how much you get to eat
Sat where I'm sat. I wanted to have a little chat
About a new direction. I know you're thinking,
What does he want? But you shouldn't suspect.
I had him in here, Silvan Shalom, with his suit and new designer lens.
Telling me what he tells tabloids,
He knows every pisher in the party.
"You can't get rid of me," he says,
"I'm too big to be left out of Finance."
"Have another one of these cigars," I said.
I understand you like cigars too, Bibi.
Would you like one? Or is Cuban too common?
You know what Ben Gurion used to say to me?
"Don't lie." Can you believe that?
As one Prime Minister to another,
Would you say that to someone who showed promise?
So what, say we cut the crap.
We know each other too well to bullshit.
Israel's economy is on the mat
And I understand you studied economics?
How about you take the Ministry of Finance
And let Silvan Shalom stretch his wings?
You don't want to go and sit outside
The state rooms I go in, where you would sit.
It's not beneath you, naturally,
But you were made for better things.
Do what you like. I'll back you up. I won't steal credit.
You come back here and tell me flat
Yes or no – I promise I won't make you regret it,
The way another Prime Minister I knew once did.
You believe that? One tiny war. He goes ballistic.

Arik and Company

I'm kidding. Just kidding.
What do you say? You want to save my illustrious tuches?

Why Then

                                                                      2005

No one can tell you the colour of his brain
or if he changed his mind, what made it bend
or if the colour purple was what he admired
when he looked on a hilltop
and saw not snipers but flowers –

No one can tell you the colour of his brain
or why Arik went from saying "No" to saying "When"
but when you look down at the cards it's his hand
Not Rabin's that left the decks cleared, door unslammed.

Why was he struck down? Because we eat ham
And every other part of a leader, until they're clean.

When

2005

When they gave back the desert
I wept a little. Who would not weep
To give up their childhood playing in sand?
I wept and I prayed and I signed my card
And said they could give it back.

When they gave back the village
I feared a little. Why, when there's so many lanes
Should the path of history always run
Through mine, where I buried my heart?
I dug up my heart and let them build.

When they came to ask for my house
My children were in the yard.
I asked if they had the right card.
They showed me where I had signed
And I could see my name had smudged.

I said, "But we live here."
They said, "Since when?"
And now when the river runs down hill
We go with it, with the rain
And I cover my children with my hands
To stop their shakes, and the wind.

Her Orange Hat

2005

Her orange hat is faded
from the sun where it burned red
and finally folded
into the sea of cooling lead.

Her anger is not what it was
more puzzled than rage
as if the bear was swatted
across the face now many days.

She came here fifteen years ago
now her son's friends cry
and see what she sees
from her TV on the yeshiva roof, the sky:

just soldiers, teenaged soldiers
carrying her dream torn limb from limb;
one soldier has a tattered scarf
one a child that cries and will not sleep –

Her son, up on that roof top
throwing acid at the guns
says he wouldn't hurt a fly
but can you ever forgive killers of flowers?

Her son, down from that roof
now facing charges, her son's friends,
somewhere a dream dies
not on a roof but down where life remains.

Her hat, its orange straw
is faded – just like a dream.
Somewhere in her son's hands
acid burns the tracks where hope sank in the seams.

A Family Picture

2005

A family picture on the wall,
A space where someone's heirloom fell
A washing line that's almost full
Some soldiers coming up the lane.

The packing started weeks ago.
First this neighbour, then that.
There was a lot of praying in the public square.
Then one by one people bought tape.

The true ones, deep
Believers still thought the Holy One Blessed be He
Would set aside his own few sheep
Would smite the soldiers with a sleep.

Somebody's cousin came in the first line.
Somebody else's brother was in uniform.
A girl who came here for a month
For seminary was back with green on her arm.

Where will I move with all these things?
A picture of a family wedding.
This space above the bedroom socket
Where she hit the wall that day when she was nine.

The Feast

2006

"*Not where he eats, but where he is eaten*" – Hamlet

The general with his blue gown on
And the tubes and tissues down his arm,
The clasp in his nose like a prize tup
And the bed tilted so he doesn't fall –

It is the bulldozer, not eating but being eaten –
A little bit here, little bit there,
A big black dog tears
And wolves tear the throat grandfather bares

There in the hospital where he stares out
And stares and stares and waits for rain
To come sweep his soldiers into power again.
Wolves rise and sit on the monitor leg,

One's dripping his jaws open over the gas and air,
Another eyeing the nurse with nice breasts
("maybe *she'll* make a morsel to keep a dog till Arik's dressed") –
The ship with Ben Gurion and Begin fighting over the mast

Sits and waits over the hospital room ceiling
Wolves flicking matches sit inside the glass
Howl and crack jokes and the rip throats
Of pretty girls with cures that never last.

Song of the Second Lebanon War

2006

Whenever I'm down
Whenever I'm blue
Whenever my critics are savage

I get in my suit
And say "Bomb me Beirut"
Just like Arik.

Whenever the bombs
Fall down on the farms
Whenever a soldier goes missing

I don't blow the horn,
Just bring down the dawn
Just like Arik.

Whenever I'm down
Whenever I'm blue
Whenever Bibi says I'm sagging

I hop in my car
And say "Find me the war"
Just like Arik.

That girl is a fool
My Vice Premier went to school
With God and knows nothing but panic

I know when I go
Leap the wall with my show
I'll be King of hell
Just like Arik.

Support

Only those with clean hands
Can look in the mirror
And say, "I have not done a thing
That would attract the comment of the generations"
But flags fly only over
The coffins of breakers of collars
Be they those who drive their carts
Through heaven, or those whose kingdom is below.
The ship with eight sails
Comes out of the mist,
Collects all those who keep the faith
And leaves those whose hands stayed unraised.
The ship with eight sails
Is manned by the dead Prime Ministers
All disagreeing where the wheel should spin
But all unanimous
Arik was dangerous
And in his coffin – full of white sheets –
Arik still bobs on the ocean –
more alive than the dead
still untouchable as oil
With the sparkle of the poisonous,
The glitter of the witch
Who can tell you the truth
If you're willing to burn for it.

Odysseus Rests

With the one carnation twinkling on his breast
he lies, a river finally at rest
frozen, as if he could again command
the hosts, but he is dead as earth.

The river runs, its pilot sleeps
there's no-one left to chart the deep
the waters lap against the ship
and no-one knows which way is east.

Odysseus lies under the snow
finally not there to throw
a hand or make another throw
of any further die – a stone.

The crickets ramble in the stream
the poets mumble and creditors scream
but there is no-one left to dream
and Odysseus floats on fire to the storm.

Once there was noise and neighs and shouts
and half the world wanted his blood
but now the sky is raining doubt
and ashes in the coffee Odysseus's tea spoon left half cloud.

Once there was some-one who could say
He will return, he knows the way,
now there is nothing left but clay
in his tank tracks and where they stopped – birds fly.

Homage to Gilad Shalit

When all around were black and blue
And primed like a hair-pin trigger
You waited, and turned the days
Into a long river

Where on your back you floated
Counting the stars of Ohio
And beside you were Ehud,
And sometimes Tzipi, finally Bibi

Finally nobody, not even your parents
Only the sound of the night sky
And the guards rattling in Arabic
Then even the sound of steps on the stairs was desired.

In the Gulag, the Pale, the street
Where a Jew's hat was knocked off the pavement,
A man who bent for his hat
Was ashamed but stayed alive with the termites.

Now the dancing stars
Speak to those on their backs saying: "You're powerful"
But the hat still rolls and rolls
And can't quite be collared

You see the same place every night
Feel the same river
And when the stars lie
Say: "When can I see my mother?"

Darkness. The same songs.
Same news in the corridor.
One day a shaft of light
And a cross in your left eye, nothing more

No one to say:
"Look how they cower"
When you hold your hands over your face
And dance for the border.

Nobody Feeds the General

I think I'll take my coffee now
Before I feed the General.
It's not feeding him like it was,
Falafel and fries at half eleven
 – not elevenses mind – just half past ten –
Now it's just clear the glass lines
That fall from the stand to his thin artery,
The endless jam of translucent cars
Following each other down the road into his coronary.
I like to go and check he isn't tangled
Or knotted or heaven forfend
Starving for a drop of Nembutal.

I think I'll sit a while
On my break with the General.
It's night, nobody comes,
Nobody goes, just the animal
Noises of the machines
Counting heartbeats, the brain signal.
Nothing to count for years
In this room, do you mind if I light up, General?
Who will even smell the smoke
After I open the air conditioner?
Who will see the CC TV
When I sit under the camera
and blow rings to the window?

I think I'll take my own
Little injection with the General.
Do you mind if I blow my mind?
You were never much for losing your control.
Just a feast, an hourly release,
This is my miniature bacchanal.
See the needle slip like it's lip to lip,
Like it's totally natural?
You and me General, we're animals.
Just you were a political animal

Me, I'm a party animal.
You were never a party animal
Though you crashed so many.
What was the name of your last one again?
Oh yeah. Forward. Backward.
Bibi is back now again.
That's how it is. A pendulum.
You go forward then backward.
I see my mother lean over the washing line
Hanging linen in the sun.
See you hold falafel in your hand
Drive it in your face like a train.
See Rabin falling with a stain
On his breast pocket the shape of the Sea of Galilee,
See Ehud Olmert going to jail,
See Barak slap Arafat's back and grin,
See him turning Tzipi Livni down
To come out shaking Bibi's hand,
Begin alone in a little flat,
Walks from the kitchen to the front room
And back again. Golda Meir putting down the phone
Refusing to call the country up to fight
The night before Yom Kippur.
I see Arafat sign, see him and Rabin hug,
See the Dolphinarium exploding,
See you fly to Jenin with that look on your mug.
See the Wall with its hundreds, thousands
Streaming like ants to eat a wedding cake.
See you walk on the Temple Mount
Waiting for the Molotov cocktails to start flying.
See you picking woollen yarmulkes
Off termites streaming out of the West Bank.
See you stand on a river of blood in the darkness
See you laughing as you pick
One falafel after another out of the spitting oil with your bare fist
To pop them in your mouth, crunch
There goes Ben Gurion, there goes Bibi – no, Bibi came back again,
Bibi's in the fire now
But I can see you stand on the river,

Will you ever walk on water again?
I see you on the river General,
Will this room ever smell clean?

Afterword: Telling Lies About the Dead

After college I arrived at Boston University for a course in playwrighting taught by Derek Walcott. Instead of the full length play or two one acts required for admission I submitted twenty poems and a three page sketch. I assumed my poems would light my way and the playlet be a formality. I heard back from Boston twice: first, I was turned down for the poetry program. Next, my papers went on to Derek Walcott. He accepted me on the basis of the three pages.

It was the final year of my drama degree. A playwright recently graduated was back and teaching a playwrighting class. On a Friday morning he told me it was my turn to have something read that Monday.

"I've got nothing,".

"You've got the weekend to write something then, haven't you?" he said.

I went home for the weekend and thought no more about it until Sunday afternoon, when I went up to my attic room and wrote, in twenty minutes, a 3 page sketch in which Sid works in an office with Sylv, under the supervision of Sir. When Sir discovers that Sid has been making a model ship in a bottle, he incites Sylv to shoot him, providing a gun. "It's an offence against our image," he says. At one point Sid is left on stage alone and tries to reach the office window to open it with a hook on a stick. He finds he cannot reach it and resumes building his model ship. The play ends with Sylv left alone on stage with the gun and a question.

Everybody wondered what it was about. Bill, who taught the class, gave a big gap-toothed grin and said one word, "Rushdie". When a couple of months later the Boston University deadline came up that's what I had to send. I arrived in Boston aged 23 with a successful writing career of 3 pages to my name and not even a copy of that to look at. I'd left my cheap Amstrad computer at home.

In Boston in 1989, Derek Walcott had written "Omeros" and it was in galleys but not published. He gave it to one of my fellow students, Daniel Bausch, to review, in galley form. ("How's my book doing Daniel?" "Very good, so far.") He had finished his master-work, in short, but not heard the world's opinion of it yet, nor been elevated to the Nobel laureate's lectern in Stockholm (that would come next year). He talked a lot about the epic that year, with no reference to himself. Two remarks that stick in my mind are that the twentieth century epic was not a poem but a novel, James Joyce's "Ulysses", in which Joyce had made his own down-trodden, provincial people an epic subject, and that the twentieth century hero was an exile, an alien within that downtrodden people, a Jew. The second remark was about how Whitman's "Song of Myself" was not an epic, but "Moby Dick" was. However, "Moby Dick fails to be the great American epic because it does not address the central American subject – the subject of race." Twain's "Huckleberry Finn" was therefore the true American epic. I asked him what he thought of Stephen Vincent Benet's "John Brown's Body" and he said he'd never read it.

Now I must make a confession. Back when I was writing 3 pages on Rushdie I was also wondering about an epic and how you would go about one today. I was walking down Ben Yehuda street in Jerusalem many years later and the sun was setting. Birds were starting to twitter in the dusk and the sky was orange. I had been living in Jerusalem for less than a year but that day became aware that something momentous had happened. Ariel Sharon, the Prime Minister of Israel had shrugged off the stories of his monumental corruption that had re-surfaced unexpectedly in the morning papers but that very night had suffered a stroke and fallen into a coma. At sunset the next day it was already evident that he would not wake up. I had written one poem, some months before, with considerable difficulty, about the disengagement from Gaza. The difficulty was that I had no purchase on the subject. It seemed important, day by day you could see the city of Jerusalem fill with ribbons – either orange or blue depending on whether you favoured the settlers or the state – and they were hung on car radio antennae, hats, the straps of ladies' handbags – anywhere you could catch a breeze to show your colours. I was nominally on the side of the state and in favour of disengagement but not passionately. I didn't wear a ribbon, could not imagine getting into conversation about it, unwise as that would have been.

Then I remembered something, we had considered looking in Maale Adumin, the artsy overgrown townlet just outside Jerusalem, and just the wrong side of the very green line of the Israeli border of 1967 which we now lived just inside of in Jerusalem. (Our house was the last one before no-man's land, next to what had been an empty valley from 1948 to 1967.) But what if we'd gone to Maale Adumim? The decision had been my wife's – I had no strong convictions either way. What if we'd gone and bought a house there? And now suddenly found we had to leave it?

That mental journey down a road not taken gave me sufficient purchase to produce a poem quickly, fluently. The side it placed me on was clearly not my own, but it spoke passionately of something that was lost. An American friend I read it to said she thought the speaker was a displaced Palestinian, not a settler. When you drop your line into the well you do not know what will be lying in wait there. But if it comes back with something you weren't expecting you probably lowered it far enough to know more than yourself.

I also wrote one essay about Sharon, trying to discern from his memoirs which way he was going to jump, how he felt about the land he was about to (maybe) give up. Reading that memoir of his sparked one poem, from a turn-of-phrase about his mother. His mother came across very clearly, the most powerful influence on his character – her wistful longing for an impossible to regain youthful possibility of becoming a doctor, and flinty subsequent refusal to compromise with either Jew or Arab on those few acres that were her compensation for a life she never had.

His mother's loneliness spoke to me, it was the loneliness of my wife in Israel, perhaps at times my own loneliness in England, though now I was theoretically 'home'. And I wrote that poem and forgot about it. Then I wrote the essay. And he fell into a coma and I walked into my wife's yeshiva building at twilight and picked up one of their course outlines and on the back of it wrote a poem called "Odysseus Rests", in five minutes. I'd written a public poem once before, back in Provincetown, when Prime Minister Rabin was shot. Both times a particular man was removed, unexpectedly, who had set in train events which now could not be anticipated with any degree of confidence in his absence. Sharon and Rabin had both effected a massive change and left mid-act.

We left Israel for England when my wife received an offer of work that solved many of her problems in Israel. From abroad, I heard the Second Lebanon War had started. From abroad, I saw how Sharon, still alive in death, hovered over the country as the new government elected in his name repeated his career low, the foray into Lebanon. At least circumstances did not conspire to repeat the massacre in Sabra and Shatilla, the single lapse of judgment he will probably be remembered for, unless there is peace one day, in which case his withdrawal from Gaza will vie with it, like a wash of yellow paint over a stain of damp, to decide the final shape of his life. The war caused me to re-visit the by now published elegy, and wonder how to extend it into a brief survey of his career. A sketch. I dug up that poem about his mother. I read more of his life. More poems came.

A friend of mine, when we lived in Jerusalem, was writing the history of the settlements in the West Bank. That book consumed him. He lost weight, the shirt over his biking shorts hung loose, his hair turned grey (greyer). It seemed as if the West Bank would find the end of him, before he found the end of the West Bank. But he finished. It was well reviewed in the New York Times. He said he'd finally managed to attract the attention of the eight hundred pound gorilla whose toe he'd been pulling. I told him he had to write the biography of Arik Sharon. He said, "Arik Sharon, that's the heart of darkness. I don't have the strength to go where you'd have to go."

Another friend, an American poet who'd selected my work in a competition, responded when I asked her to support this project: "I wonder what makes you think I know so little about Sharon? I know quite a bit, and know people who worked for him during his early career of slaughter and bare-handed torture, and don't find him "morally ambiguous." I consider him an animal in human form, the closest thing to pure evil this world can produce. A kind of out-of-control Karl Rove or Dick Cheney—neither of whom killed prisoners by strangling them with their own bare hands. I don't see how one could read poems about such a monster—however tragic or complex the causes of his monstrosity—without knowing something about him."

We live in England now, in a small town of unusually liberal leanings. I was going to a poetry slam and proposed to read a poem about Sabra and Shatilla. My wife said, "Do you want us to have to leave this house? Do you want us to get bricks thrown through our window, all sorts?"

It's a strange thing writing an epic, in this day and age. Strange even to write a narrative in verse, or a series of poems, about a life not quite your own which you posit as a mirror to reflect your world. The second time I alluded in conversation to a story about Sharon's mother running in the night, in bare feet, to cut down the steel wires that demarcated where her land was going to be forcibly donated by her village to new arrivals – my wife looked at me and said, "You know why I don't like that story, don't you? They're *your* parents. I can completely imagine your mother doing that." It had never crossed my mind. But it was too late. The self-portrait was unconscious enough to have taken in the paper, and now the negative would have to be left in the dark to develop.

Writing an epic was a means for Joyce and Walcott to retain the world they'd both fled from to achieve success. I reluctantly came to see that being outside of Israel made a long poem on Sharon possible. Undoubtedly in the panic of newsflashes describing a war any longer poem would not have been possible. Epic is what you write when birds are no longer singing, guns not throwing large bales of plastic sheeting onto metal lorry bases in the ravine outside your house. Epic is the view back into a city you no longer occupy. Sometimes you can see a dome gleaming and in the bloody courtyard at its feet, a man. Sometimes in that man's hand you can see a gun, and where he's pointing it is where the guns will fire, a long time after he is gone.

A book I read after I finished writing the poem was Gilad Sharon's memoir of his father. It was too panegyric to suit my purposes but included a detail, the fact that Sharon's children often referred to his mother by drumming on the table to simulate the sound of Genghis Khan's raiding horsemen sweeping across the Steppes where she was born. That single image conjures up everything about who Sharon is and why he is a metaphor for Israel. If you wrote about Rabin you would lose sight of the fact he opened fire on the Altalena and somehow depict him as Isaiah's suffering servant, someone who died for peace. If you write about Sharon you necessarily follow a skinny guerrilla fighter who winds up very fat across the middle and personally owning a lot of real-estate, just like the State of Israel. And of course, his mother was Genghis Khan. Do you need me to draw you a picture?

Acknowledgments

"Latrun", "First Born" and "Step Into the Yard" won the 2008 War Poetry Contest and were published by Winning Writers.
"When" won the Daniel Varoujan award from the New England Poetry Club.
"Because" and "Prelude" won a Paumanok poetry award.
"Homage to Gilad Shalit" appeared in *Phai'tude,*.
"The Desert Rat" appeared in *Black Rabbit Quarterly*
"Rabin" appeared in *Jewcy*.
"A Knife in the Hand" appeared in *Sanctuary*.
"The Explosion" appeared in *Prairie Schooner*.
"Odysseus Rests" appeared in *Jewish Quarterly*

About the Author

Atar Hadari's play have been staged in New York, London, Leeds and Los Angeles. He is the author of *Rembrandt's Bible* and *Gethsemane* as well as the translator of *Songs from Bialik* and *Lives of the Dead: Collected Poems of Hanoch Levin*. Born in Israel and raised in England, he lived in Israel during the Intifada, Sharon's premiership and Disengagement. All but one of these poems is based on historical records.

The Jewish Poetry Project

jpoetry.us

Ben Yehuda Press

From the Coffee House of Jewish Dreamers: Poems of Wonder and Wandering and the Weekly Torah Portion by Isidore Century

"Isidore Century is a wonderful poet. His poems are funny, deeply observed, without pretension." —*The Jewish Week*

The House at the Center of the World: Poetic Midrash on Sacred Space by Abe Mezrich

"Direct and accessible, Mezrich's midrashic poems often tease profound meaning out of his chosen Torah texts. These poems remind us that our Creator is forgiving, that the spiritual and physical can inform one another, and that the supernatural can be carried into the everyday."
—Yehoshua November, author of *God's Optimism*

we who desire:
Poems and Torah riffs by Sue Swartz

"Sue Swartz does magnificent acrobatics with the Torah. She takes the English that's become staid and boring, and adds something that's new and strange and exciting. These are poems that leave a taste in your mouth, and you walk away from them thinking, what did I just read? Oh, yeah. It's the Bible."
—Matthue Roth, author, *Yom Kippur A Go-Go*

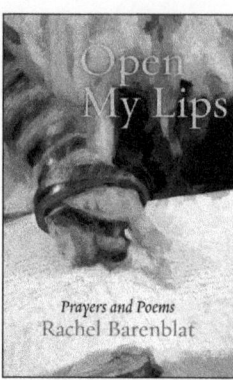

Open My Lips: Prayers and Poems by Rachel Barenblat

"Barenblat's God is a personal God—one who lets her cry on His shoulder, and who rocks her like a colicky baby. These poems bridge the gap between the ineffable and the human. This collection will bring comfort to those with a religion of their own, as well as those seeking a relationship with some kind of higher power."
—Satya Robyn, author, *The Most Beautiful Thing*

Words for Blessing the World: Poems in Hebrew and English by Herbert J. Levine

"These writings express a profoundly earth-based theology in a language that is clear and comprehensible. These are works to study and learn from."
—Rodger Kamenetz, author, *The Jew in the Lotus*

Shiva Moon: Poems by Maxine Silverman

"The poems, deeply felt, are spare, spoken in a quiet but compelling voice, as if we were listening in to her inner life. This book is a precious record of the transformation saying Kaddish can bring. It deserves to be read."
—Howard Schwartz, author, *The Library of Dreams*

is: heretical Jewish blessings and poems by Yaakov Moshe (Jay Michaelson)

"Finally, Torah that speaks to and through the lives we are actually living: expanding the tent of holiness to embrace what has been cast out, elevating what has been kept down, advancing what has been held back, reveling in questions, revealing contradictions."
—Eden Pearlstein, aka eprhyme

Texts to the Holy: Poems
by Rachel Barenblat

"These poems are remarkable, radiating a love of God that is full bodied, innocent, raw, pulsating, hot, drunk. I can hardly fathom their faith but am grateful for the vistas they open. I will sit with them, and invite you to do the same."
—Merle Feld, author of *A Spiritual Life*

The Sabbath Bee: Love Songs to Shabbat
by Wilhelmina Gottschalk

"Torah, say our sages, has seventy faces. As these prose poems reveal, so too does Shabbat. Here we meet Shabbat as familiar housemate, as the child whose presence transforms a family, as a spreading tree, as an annoying friend who insists on being celebrated, as a woman, as a man, as a bee, as the ocean."
—Rachel Barenblat, author, *The Velveteen Rabbi's Haggadah*

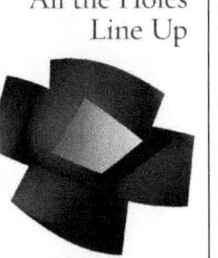

All the Holes Line Up: Poems and Translations
by Zackary Sholem Berger

"Spare and precise, Berger's poems gaze unflinchingly at—but also celebrate—human imperfection in its many forms. And what a delight that Berger also includes in this collection a handful of his resonant translations of some of the great Yiddish poets."
—Yehoshua November, author of *God's Optimism* and *Two Worlds Exist*

How to Bless the New Moon:
Songs of the Sovereign and the Icon
by Rachel Kann

"Rachel Kann is a master wordsmith. Her poems are rich in content, packed with life's wisdom and imbued with soul. May this collection of her work enable more of the world to enjoy her offerings."
—Sarah Yehudit Schneider, author of *You Are What You Hate*

Into My Garden: Prayers
by David Caplan

"The beauty of Caplan's book is that it is not polemical. It does not set out to win an argument or ask you whether you've put your tefillin on today. These gentle poems invite the reader into one person's profound, ambiguous religious experience."
— *The Jewish Review of Books*

Between the Mountain and the Land is the Lesson: Poetic Midrash on Sacred Community by Abe Mezrich

"Abe Mezrich cuts straight back to the roots of the Midrashic tradition, sermonizing as a poet, rather than ideologue. Best of all, Abe knows how to ask questions and avoid the obvious answers."
—Jake Marmer, author, *Jazz Talmud*

NOKADDISH: Poems in the Void
by Hanoch Guy Kaner

"A subversive, midrashic play with meanings–specifically Jewish meanings, and then the reversal and negation of these meanings."
—Robert G. Margolis

An Added Soul: Poems for a New Old Religion
by Herbert J. Levine

"Herbert J. Levine's lovely poems swing wide the double doors of English and Hebrew and open on the awe of being. Clear and direct, at ease in both tongues, these lyrics embrace a holiness unyoked from myth and theistic searching."
—Lynn Levin, author, *The Minor Virtues*

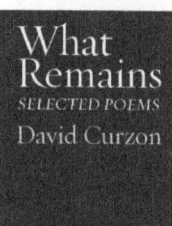

What Remains
by David Curzon

"Aphoristic, ekphrastic, and precise revelations animate WHAT REMAINS. In his stunning rewriting of Psalm 1 and other biblical passages, Curzon shows himself to be a fabricator, a collector, and an heir to the literature, arts, and wisdom traditions of the planet."
—Alicia Ostriker, author of *The Volcano and After*

The Shortest Skirt in Shul
by Sass Oron

"These poems exuberantly explore gender, Torah, the masks we wear, and the way our bodies (and the ways we wear them) at once threaten stable narratives, and offer the kind of liberation that saves our lives."
—Alicia Jo Rabins, author of *Divinity School*, composer of *Girls In Trouble*

Walking Triptychs
by Ilya Gutner

These are poems from when I walked about Shanghai and thought about the meaning of the Holocaust.

Book of Failed Salvation
by Julia Knobloch

"These beautiful poems express a tender longing for spiritual, physical, and emotional connection. They detail a life in movement—across distances, faith, love, and doubt."
—David Caplan, author, *Into My Garden*

Daily Blessings: Poems on Tractate Berakhot
by Hillel Broder

"Hillel Broder does not just write poetry about the Talmud; he also draws out the Talmud's poetry, finding lyricism amidst legality and re-setting the Talmud's rich images like precious gems in end-stopped lines of verse."
—Ilana Kurshan, author of *If All the Seas Were Ink*

The Red Door: A dark fairy tale told in poems
by Shawn C. Harris

"THE RED DOOR, like its poet author Shawn C. Harris, transcends genres and identities. It is an exploration in crossing worlds. It brings together poetry and story telling, imagery and life events, spirit and body, the real and the fantastic, Jewish past and Jewish present, to spin one tale." —Einat Wilf, author, *The War of Return*

The Missing Jew: Poems 1976-2022
by Rodger Kamenetz

"How does Rodger Kamenetz manage to have so singular a voice and at the same time precisely encapsulate the world view of an entire generation (also mine) of text-hungry American Jews born in the middle of the twentieth century?"
—Jacqueline Osherow, author, *Ultimatum from Paradise* and *My Lookalike at the Krishna Temple: Poems*

The Matter of Families
by Robert H. Deluty

"Robert Deluty's career-spanning collection of New and Selected poems captures the essence of his work: the power of love, joy, and connection, all tied together with the poet's glorious sense of humor. This book is Deluty's masterpiece."
—Richard M. Berlin, M.D., author of *Freud on My Couch*

There Is No Place Without You
by Maya Bernstein

"Bernstein's poems brim with energy and sound, moving the reader around a world mapped by motherhood, contemplation, religion, and the effects of illness on the body and spirit. Her language is lyrical, delicate, and poised; her lens is lucid and original."
—Anthony Anaxagorou, author of *After the Formalities*

Torah Limericks
by Rhonda Rosenheck

"Rhonda Rosenheck knows the Hebrew Bible, and she knows that it can stand up to the sometimes silly, sometimes snarky, but always insightful scholarship packed into each one of these interpretive jewels."
—Rabbi Hillel Norry

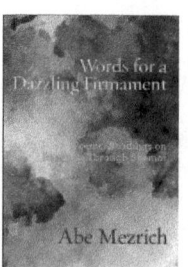

Words for a Dazzling Firmament
by Abe Mezrich

"Mezrich is a cultivated craftsman: interpretively astute, sonically deliberate, and spiritually cunning."

—Zohar Atkins, author of *Nineveh*

Everything Thaws
by R. B. Lemberg

"Full of glacier-sharp truths, and moments revealed between words like bodies beneath melting permafrost. As it becomes increasingly plain how deeply our world is shaped by war and climate change and grief and anger, articulating that shape feels urgent and necessary."
—Ruthanna Emrys, author of *A Half-Built Garden*

Ode to the Dove: *An illustrated, bilingual edition of a Yiddish poem by Abraham Sutzkever*
Zackary Sholem Berger, translator
Liora Ostroff, Illustrator

"An elegant volume for lovers of poetry."
—Justin Cammy, translator of *Sutzkever, From the Vilna Ghetto to Nuremberg: Memoir and Testimony*

Poems for a Cartoon Mouse
by Andrew Burt

"Andrew Burt's poetry magnifies the vanishingly small line between danger and safety. This collection asks whether order is an illusion that veils chaos, or vice-versa, juxtaposing images from the Bible with animated films."
—Ari Shapiro, host of NPR's *All Things Considered*

Old Shul
by Pinny Bulman

"Nostalgia gives way to a tender theology, a softly chuckling illumination from within the heart of/as a beautiful, broken sanctuary, somehow both gritty and fragile, grimy and iridescent – not unlike faith itself."
—Jake Marmer, author of *Cosmic Diaspora*

Feet In L.A., But My Womb Lives In Jerusalem, My Breath In Vermont
by Lori Levy

"Takes my breath away. With no pretense whatsoever, they leap, alive, from the page until this reader felt as if she were living Levy's life. How does the author do it?"
—Mary Jo Balistreri, author of *Still*

Poem Hashavuah
by Lexie Botzum and Jessica Spencer

"This collection illuminates the white fire of the Torah — the ancient and modern literary interpretations that carve out the negative space of the Torah's letters so that they dance before us as joyously as when they were given in fire on Sinai."
—Ilana Kurshan, author of *If All the Seas Were Ink*

Bits and Pieces
by Edward Pomerantz

"A natural dramatist who looks back on his life growing up in Washington Heights in a series of vivid vignettes inspired by his early moviegoing."
—Robert Vas Dias, author of *Poetics Of Still Life: A Collage*

Not Akhmatova
by Noah Berlatsky

"In these poems, Noah Berlatsky approaches the work of Anna Akhmatova—or scrambles off in another direction entirely. Writing under the sign of her name, with her but without trying to become her, Berlatsky gives us Anna in transcreation, in transelation."
—Sarah Dowling, author of *Entering Sappho*

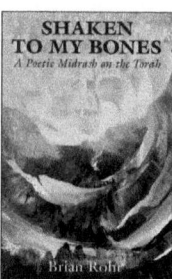
Shaken to My Bones
by Brian Rohr

"In Brian Rohr's exquisite poems, wonders unfold. We are taken along on a journey both ancient and immediate — one that is rewarding beyond comparison."
—Baruch November, author of *Bar Mitzvah Dreams*

So Many Warm Words: Selections from the Poetry of Rosa Nevadovska, translated by Merle L. Bachman

"This bilingual edition makes Nevadovska's oeuvre—poems of loneliness and longing countered by others expressing joyous moments of transcendence—accessible, for the first time, to the English reader."
—Sheva Zucker, editor emerita of *Afn Shvel*.

The Whole Mishpocha
by Philip Terman

"Gathers the Jewish-themed poems of an accomplished poet who has been producing memorable work on the Jewish-American experience for decades. I have long admired Terman's exceptional poems for their Jewish ethos, beautiful lyricism, and emotional risk taking."
—Yehoshua November, author of *God's Optimism*

Styx by Else Lasker-Schüler
translated by Mildred Faintly

"Reborn in Mildred Faintly's magnificent translation, Else Lasker-Schüler's STYX overflows with shudders of desolation, moans of sexual pleasure, ecstatic fusions of love and despite that exalt and torture in equal measure."
—Joy Ladin, author of *The Book of Anna* and *Shekhinah Speaks.*

Chrysalis Summer
by Suzanne Brody

"We are invited into the thoughts and emotions of one woman who plays many roles—teacher, mother, rabbi, and artist. Topics stretch from the mundane business of cleaning up students' glitter to weightier topics such as egalitarianism and Biblical texts."
—Dori Weinstein, author of the *YaYa & YoYo* series *Considered*

Blessed Are You, Wondrous Universe:
A Siddur for Seekers by Herbert J. Levine

"Herb Levine has fashioned a sparkling collection of prayers for a thinking, feeling modern person who wants to express gratitude for the wonder of existence."
—Daniel Matt, translator of the Zohar, author of *God and the Big Bang*, *The Essential Kabbalah*, and *Becoming Elijah*

Animals are Shouting Down from the Sky
by Genevieve Greinetz

"Often heart-stopping, these poems abound in images uniquely unfamiliar. Not intended for the casual reader, they capture the violation of nature, free speech silenced, humanity flattened, families – and friends – failing as they often do."
—Merle Feld, author of *Longing, Poems for a Life*

www.ingramcontent.com/pod-product-compliance
Lightning Source LLC
LaVergne TN
LVHW041343080426
835512LV00006B/596